Schools
Past and Present

by Kerry Dinmont

BUMBA BOOKS™

LERNER PUBLICATIONS ◆ MINNEAPOLIS

Note to Educators:

Throughout this book, you'll find critical thinking questions. These can be used to engage young readers in thinking critically about the topic and in using the text and photos to do so.

Lerner Publications Company
A division of Lerner Publishing Group, Inc.
241 First Avenue North
Minneapolis, MN 55401 USA

For reading levels and more information, look up this title at www.lernerbooks.com.

Library of Congress Cataloging–in–Publication Data

Names: Dinmont, Kerry, 1982– author.
Title: Schools past and present / Kerry Dinmont.
Description: Minneapolis : Lerner Publications, 2018. | Series: Bumba books. Past and present | Includes bibliographical references and index. | Audience: Age 4–7. | Audience: K to Grade 3.
Identifiers: LCCN 2017058427 (print) | LCCN 2017051931 (ebook) | ISBN 9781541507777 (eb pdf) | ISBN 9781541503298 (lb : alk. paper) | ISBN 9781541526907 (pb)
Subjects: LCSH: Schools—Juvenile literature. | Schools—History—Juvenile literature.
Classification: LCC LB1556 (print) | LCC LB1556 .D56 2018 (ebook) | DDC 371—dc23

LC record available at https://lccn.loc.gov/2017058427

Manufactured in the United States of America
1 – CG – 7/15/18

Table of
Contents

School through History

School is a fun place

to learn.

It has changed

through history.

In the past, school lasted

only a few years.

Children go to school for

longer now.

Why do you think school used to last just a few years?

Kids who were done with school did

chores at home.

Many worked on family farms.

These days, many kids still do chores

at home.

But they also do homework.

Schools used to have

one room.

Children of all ages

learned together.

A school today has many classrooms. Grades are usually separate.

Why do you think schools separate kids by age?

Students used to write on chalkboards.

Today many schools have computers.

Students walked to school

in the past.

Today some students still

walk to school.

Others take a bus or car.

Schools today are very different from the past.

How do the changes help you learn?

Then and Now

Then	Today
Children went to school for a few years.	Children go to school for a longer time.
Schools had one room.	Schools have many rooms.
Students wrote on chalkboards.	Students use computers.

Picture Glossary

chalkboards

boards that can be written on with chalk

chores

daily jobs in a home or on a farm

grades

students of the same age at a school

separate

not kept together

Read More

Parkes, Elle. *Hooray for Teachers!* Minneapolis: Lerner Publications, 2017.

Reinke, Beth Bence. *School Buses on the Go.* Minneapolis: Lerner Publications, 2018.

Slade, Suzanne. *With Books and Bricks: How Booker T. Washington Built a School.* Chicago: Albert Whitman & Company, 2014.

Index

Photo Credits